Musings in Quarter Time

Anne Buster

BookLeaf
Publishing

India | USA | UK

Musings in Quarter Time © 2023 Anne Buster

All rights reserved.

Presentation by *BookLeaf Publishing*

Web: www.bookleafpub.com

E-mail: info@bookleafpub.com

ISBN: 9789358369472

First edition 2023

Free time keeps me going. - Gus Van Sant

*1

The dog dug up the carrots today,
And carrots take forever to grow.
If it had been radishes I wouldn't care as much
But it couldn't have been.
The radishes would have been harvested long
ago
Unlike the stubborn carrots
But who wouldn't choose a carrot over a radish?
We wait longer because they are sweeter, easier
and that only comes with time.
I replant the dug up bits of green with white
taproots that search in the earth.
The dog, I bring inside.
He wants what he wants, dirt on his paws,
the warmth of the house, table scraps
just as the carrot wants to carve its spot in the
soil.
A shock of orange treasure, sweeter than any
radish.

*2

I sit around and read poetry and wait for you.
To do your homework
Notice the cat's bowl is empty
Hang up your towel
Walk the dogs
Clean out your backpack
It becomes a scale
Which weighs more the waiting or the doing
I do too much
But if I don't you are just a void
You care about movies and TV
Chatting with friends over the interwebs
Digging in mud like a four year old
There's a reason it's your favorite number
I am waiting for you.
To develop like a photo in a darkroom
To understand responsibility
To grow up
It becomes an anchor that I drag around
The weight of what you should do or what you
can do - which should I carry?
I do too little
But if I do more I am a void.
You care about me, animals, the green earth
Eating and hiking

You are old for your years, young for your size
I am waiting for you.
Please come to me.

***3**

We belong to the world and
the world belongs to us,
Though most of the time it doesn't act like it.
It acts like a dog, not trained for its leash,
That rockets sideways claiming no allegiance to
anyone,
yet tied to us all the same.

Our lives are not our own.

We say we are tired
because it is easier to say tired than
I am overwhelmed by the heaviness and
complexity of life.

We ask how are you?
As a paltry offering of commiseration.
We don't really care but we want to and
we want the world to think that we do.

The world, that bad dog that sometimes comes
with growls and bites
and sometimes leans in and puts its head in your
lap,
as if to say:
Underneath it all I have always loved you.

*4

Tie the tomato seedlings to stakes
And talk to your goddaughter about her future
Like you know what you are doing
Like we aren't all just shooting in the dark

Garden at night
And you get rewarded with mosquito bitten feet
Is there anything poetic about being itchy?
Talk to the better boys and early girls, coax the
mortgage lifters into fruition.
Thank you but we know how to be tomatoes,
they say.

Your son walks the dog and you hang at the
window like a girl waiting for her date. Worry is
a shadow, a fruit fly, an unwanted companion.

Better to be like a tomato, so sure of yourself.
I cut one and make a sandwich, anything to keep
my hands busy.

*5

The children on the yard run in all directions
They remind me of a meteor shower
Arcing out unpredictably

The dog ate a bird
We visit the new school
Drive the 10 again
The radio makes us question the government,
the country, the future
Spread thin
The endless running and then waiting
Catering and planning
How like childhood is old age- I buy diapers
again,
get a picture book to keep her busy.
I just want to look at the light through the palm
trees
To write my little poems
To not feel like I must worry in order to survive

*6

Twice I've lost you,
Like a misplaced shoe or receipt.
You who are everything,
Wandered off at the beach,
Took a wrong path hiking.
Lost for a moment.
I knew I would get you back, would hold you
again and comfort you.
Yet it hurt like a string tightening in my chest,
How could I be so careless?
You who are everything,
Who things hurt more for,
who remembers the worst things always and the
best things only sometimes, who is plagued by
the hungry chasm of your thoughts
I cannot afford to fail you
And yet it is in the nature of my human ness -
failure . ineptitude . thoughtlessness
You who are everything
Do you know how sick I feel when I cannot help
you?
My gut wrenched, chest tight, scared.
Someday you will be free, and far away
And still the feeling will persist.

Lips dry, heart in my tight throat, holding back
tears.
I will always be waiting with open arms for
You who are everything.

*7

The lines on my hands are changing
Did I make the right choice?
The lines change whether you do or not
What's right anyway?

These furrows speak of life and love
Not the last conversation with your mother
Or the way his arm looped round your shoulders
at the fireworks show for the first time, taller
than you.

Lines don't mean a thing
We cross them constantly
But are they a map?
Look there where this triangle is forming that's
joy,
hold it tight in your wrinkled hand.

*8

On the ranch
The grand pleasure of animals
Goats and sheep and horses and donkeys
A fat pig, a tiny kitten, a soulful dog large as a
pony.

I cannot contain my delight in these beasts
Their simple being, their purposefulness, how
much they want what they want - all the creature
comforts of their four legged life.

Why do we make it so hard? They demand
snacks and affection-
they bray and holler and grunt at each other and
at us - and we laugh,
We give them what they want
And they give us delight.

*9

What we sometimes are- this synchronicity
It carries through
all the times we are something else-
The laborious joylessness of mornings
Eternal conversations about food
The stories about the people at the market,
the monotony of money, the planning of travel,
So much television, the hot tub, night at the
Bowl, tacos from a new place,
did you run the dishwasher, feed the dogs

But Sometimes we are copacetic, attuned and
teasing,
given to secret language, kind familiarity -
the long days and short years all saying
I think you are really something.

*10

Look at stars and clouds,
the branches of trees,
the bird perched on the line
singing singing
Eat ripe fruit in season
Pet the cat until his body relaxes on you
like he has poured himself on to my lap,
a wet noodle feline
Walk the dog and see his happy bouncing ears
Read until the light changes in the sky and the
world vanishes
See the milk cloud and expand in my tea
Watch the ginkgo green and then yellow again
Enjoy the passage of time
Enjoy quiet
I want the simple, the here and now, nothing
fancy.
Cut me this slice of pie and I'll eat it cheerfully,
exuberantly,
never once thinking of Cake.

*11

I want my feelings to fit together
Instead life stalls and then revs like an old car
So fast and then the slow that goes on and on
I want The story that I tell myself to be a line not
a squiggle

We grow slow
Not as fast as trees, who are always striving
towards the sun - instead
Slowly we double-back and try again
Bending and reshaping ourselves
To grow through the odds instead of against
them

Matching what you want to need with what you
actually do,
realizing that memories are perhaps crafted lies,
that the only way to fill the sky and spread your
branches is uncertainty.
And trust - so much trust.

*12

Watch the crows walk across the road
like angry gentlemen late to a meeting
full of avian purpose
The sun glints on a bit of trash
a candy wrapper bright as light on an ocean
wave

Is this noticing the bridge to joy?
Laugh at the crows in the road,
drink in the morning,
it's what we've got.

*13

All the time I'm judging
My melancholic voice
My lazy parenting
How easy it is to sit and watch TV and pretend
that is an evening
Just keeping time
Judge the house
my shortcomings
the rigors I can't keep up
How much I can sleep
how I yearn to be alone
Judge it all and then turn again
try to remember to be kind to yourself, whatever
that means
to hold yourself
to be proud
Pick up and work again with all your feelings.
How we carry on is the great mystery.
At least most of us are not Fredric Thomas'
crickets,
drowning ourselves to feed the parasite inside.
We struggle inelegantly but survive
meet the day

If only one could meet it with forgiveness

of all our shortcomings, the things you should
have said
the laziness that is actually fatigue

Just meet the day (not seize it)
That will do.

$$*14$$

17

How do you recover from anything?
Pandemic, death, illness, anger,
the darkness that gathers and solidifies.

How you watch people change even as they
claim they are static
How you watch yourself change -
and become unimaginable,
a destination never charted.

I built a fortress around my mind and now it all
collects
Like silt dammed up, thick with murky clouds
How do you break what you build?

*15

Taxed with illness and graced with height
the hours are easy with you
Lets make everything a joke
Share arcane facts
You are blithe about God and meaning
Yet down deep you see the divine in animals
The web of narrative
You hate humans but love their creation
The open worlds, the hero's journey,
the tropes that become part of your own story
You eat history, enjoy conversation
You cannot imagine a hard path
even though yours is hard
The force of you is like a plow
see how I make this road by walking
The world is not your oyster but perhaps your
apple
Here hanging from the low branch
Sweet and tart like you.

*16

Everyday threatens to eat me alive
Delete me from my life
There are tasks calling
The roles you choose
and those thrust on you
The song of the leaf is so quiet

I want joy and laughter and warm blue nights
The taste of salt on skin
The smell of the first lemon
The shock that joy can still find you
even after heart break
even after the losses that yawn to devour you

Don't let them.

Look at the leaf that beats against the window
even as your heart beats
find within you an invincible Spring
not the glaring heat and pride of summer
but the humbleness of a small bud on a
seemingly dead branch -
the life within you that clamors to exist again.

*17

How you gathered me up and held me in the
rocking chair
The table from the old Boston library
The TV always on -
Carson, Hart to Hart, Moonlighting, Masterpiece
Theater
The brown-orange rug
The Catholic Reporter and the LA Times by
your chair
How angry they made you -
(the news even then a sorrow song about the
world circling the drain)
Your Birkenstocks, the zippered jacket
Iced coffee every summer long before Starbucks

Your journals, the Maltin movie guide
Climbing into your bed to wake you in the
afternoon.
Joan Baez and Paul Simon on the phonograph
Singing with the radio - Temptations, Unchained
Melody, The Lion Sleep Tonight
Indian skirts, the laughter that always followed
your comments

Swimming in the pool, in the ocean, in the bay

Long laps while you told me myths
Holding my arm as we go to the movies
The bridge in Venice where you begged me to
remember happiness
Toothpaste on your shirt
Wine
Watching the oscars
The smell of furniture polish and tea rose
perfume when we had company
Reading aloud
Notes and postcards from you in the mail
One thousand three eared rabbits
Jewelry from the museum
Talking and talking
Cards - playing spite and malice
The lives of the saints
Noxema
Mister the dog
Dick and his apple
Mom's accusing cigarette glinting in the dark
driving fast on the 405 late at night
Campbell's books
car hopping at the A&W
working as a waitress in the only Mexican
restaurant in Charlottesville
The "pretty park" where you took my brother to
play in a graveyard
Staying up late
Potato chips with mayonnaise

Artichokes
Peter Rabbit by moonlight on a bench in Mexico

It's bits and pieces,
A million warm thoughts,
That I have instead of having you.

*18

The dead go on living with us
It's said what is lost can't be restored
But the wormy tomatoes are plowed into the soil
and the birds nest in the dead tree
We read the thoughts of the dead and become
changed
Our minds forever carrying them with us

The dead go on living with us
It's best to set them a place at the table
But if you don't you honor them anyway
You preserve them just by being
Inhale deeply
You are breathing for so many

$$*19$$

Named for a monster, a myth
You are protector
Both shield and to be shielded

Your laughter is contagious
(I thought that was just something people said
until I felt how freely my laughter followed
yours.)
It burbles out of you like an undammed creek.

All that you feel is writ large
Eager to please
Hard headed as an unbroken horse
Kind heart, you love hard
Thoughtful and full of promise
Will you strive to be more?
Will you break away?

*20

You sat on the desk in your dress shirt and tie
and told the girls of Hamlet
How character is destiny

You made me pancakes shaped like animals
Summer mornings just the two of us
Maybe a trip to the Egg and the Eye

At pickup, at the market, at the doctor, at the
wheel driving cross country, reading aloud at
night every voice in Dickens, making dinner
it was always you

How infinite the chapters of your knowledge
a history of trains,
reciting poetry from memory,
ship wrecks of the 19th century
the actors in pre-code films
I can't learn it all

We had consistency instead of magic -
a stability that built my life
You were steadfast

There is your words, notes from former students,
your studies, articles by you that will be read
years from now, books you were thanked in.

For me there is the kitchen in the apartment I
grew up in,
your arms holding me as you cook eggs, your
wool bathrobe rough on my cheek, the smell of
coffee on you like cologne.
A solidness that can't fade.

*21

Wonder is a comfort.
The questions can't be answered.
Order exists and expands beyond our
understanding.

Bats hear shapes
And trees are made of fractals
Math and poetry melt out of everything

Bees dance in maps
perhaps we do too
What we can't see can shape us and hold us
together
Sticky as honey and just as sweet.